Verse to Reverse
the Classroom Blues

Mike Kivi
with illustrations by Bill Stott

tb

Trentham Books

First published in 1993 by Trentham Books Limited

Trentham Books Limited
Westview House
734 London Road
Oakhill, Stoke-on-Trent
England ST4 5NP

British Library Cataloguing in Publication Data
A catalogue record for this book is available at the British
Library.

ISBN: 0 948080 94 9

With grateful acknowledgements to *Education Magazine,
The Teacher, Headlines, The Times Educational Supplement*
and many other journals, etc.

Designed and typeset by Trentham Print Design, Ltd
and printed by Bemrose Shafron Ltd, Chester.

For Dad

Contents

Foreword *by Mitch Howard*   9

'The English are rather a foul mouthed nation'   11
antiphony   12
From Reason to Treason   13
Flora Electora   14
Sic Sic   15
The Ballad of Cool Hand Smith   16
My Vote   18
The Raving Loony's Charter   19
What the Thunder Said (The Survivors)   20

Begone dull care   21
C. A Valediction   22
The Peste   24
Pass the Cocoa Ken   26

Nuts in April   27
A Seaside Medley   28
The Winter Gardens Tale   29

... lastly through a hogshead of real fire   31
God's Messenger   32
Nunc Dimittis   33
Death by Soft Soap   35
The White Paper — a Deymystification   36

Why *not* shoot the messenger?   37
The Last Flight of the Shire Fighter   38
Who's Who?   39
Jazz   41
Shakespeare in Schools   43

School is for Kids too 45
Syllabus A 46
Another of Life's Sweet Mysteries 47
Performance Art 48
Now we are theven (muthic) 49
PSE Poem 50

Summer Relief 51
The unofficial opening of the football season 52
Overheard on the Beach 54
A Postcard from Devon 55
Overheard on the Beach (2) 56
September is the saddest month 57
Thermal Verse 58
Withdrawal Method 59
Back to Maastricht 60
September Assignment 62
Theven and a bit 63
Lingua Peripatetica 64
Via Triviale 65
a right royal poem 66

True Stories 67
Response (to Adrian Henri's inclusion on the 1994 English 68
Literature Syllabus)
Reathonth for Reading 69
Teachers I have known 70
The Baker's Tale 71
Footy Poem for the Fourth Term 72

'God bless, us one and all' 73
Santa Clarke's Last Visit 74
Advent 76
Christmas at Sea or The Wreck of The Gerbil 77
The first daze of Christmas 84
Old Major's Christmas Message 85

Foreword

Mitch Howard — Editor, The Teacher

I held the plain brown envelope gingerly. There were poems in it, I was told. Not just any old poems but poems about teaching written by a teacher hoping for publication in where else? *The Teacher.* Fearing the worst, I let time and tide carry their unopened envelope away from the epicentre of my desk top to the far-flung outer reaches. The weeks went by until one day the Good Ship Brown Envelope of Really Funny Poems All About Teaching reached the end of its world and promptly fell over the edge.

This was clearly a Sign. I owed it to this bloke Kivi to at least look at his poems. I picked up the envelope and pulled out the sheets of what was to become *Potent Poems for Pole Axed Pedagogues.* Already I was composing the letter: 'The poems are very interesting and I enjoyed reading many of them, however I regret that they are not suitable...'.

How wrong I was. I read them, I enjoyed them, and *The Teacher* has regularly published Mike's poems ever since. Before long Mike and I found ourselves hacking a too-long epic over the phone until it fitted the space on the page: 'How about dropping the fifth stanza except for the last two lines which we could tag on the end of the seventh?' I was impressed — not least because it was my fault. I'd given Mike the wrong length. Here was no prima donna hung up on the right to life of his every word but a craftsman with a sense of humour — in the best tradition of Big Bill himself, I shouldn't wonder.

Now another bunch of Kivi fruit has ripened. Most of *Verse to Reverse the Classroom Blues* is about teaching but Mike's technique lends itself just as well to politicians and elections as sad-faced chalkies and the NUT in seaside conference mode. And if in this second volume I detect less emphasis on pastiche and more on content, perhaps this is because there's not an awful lot in education to laugh about right now.

Mike's poems strike chords in staffrooms around the country. Who knows, he could become so popular that he receives the ultimate kiss of death for a living poet and becomes a set text: 'It is at once Kivi's triumph and his failure that pastiche is his chosen vehicle to convey a post-modernist synthesis of art and life in the 1990s.' Discuss with reference to Maastricht, miners and Madonna.

In the meantime I urge you to get out your Kivi — and never to ignore a plain brown envelope.

'The English are rather a foul mouthed nation'
— Hazlett

antiphony

atlantis rises in the east
by satellite and star,
foundation of arabia's peace,
the frankincense bazaar;
a culture's base, a mystic source,
the orient's perfection,
while in the west our gods have blessed
a general election.

From Reason to Treason

Now all day long they sift electoral rolls,
From marginal to safely guarded seat,
Divining in the entrails of the polls
Fresh evidence of victory and defeat.
Now comes the *Tory* with his aided school,
The *Raving Loony* and the gentle *Green*,
The *Socialist* with County Council rule,
The reasoned *Liberal* somewhere in between.

Some call for teaching children in the mass
While others cry that forty is too much,
Protesting the iniquities of class,
A paradox exemplified by *Sutch*.
Bold critics of the liberal Plowden years
Betray acute infection's fevered voice.
With scarcely hidden xenophobic fears
And logic tortured by the use of *Choice*.

The whiplash from the ministerial tongue
Cracks out against the *Socialist* complaint,
And bland assurance leads the heady song
Of *Democratic* caution and restraint.
The nonsense flows from *Journalist* and *Don*
From *Union* left and *National Party* right,
The siren voices prate and garble on
From morning news till after dark at night.

Old *Kinnock* throws his manifesto down,
Pulls back the formal infant classroom screen,
While five o-levelled *Major* casts a frown
And *Ashdown* lingers somewhere in between.
Apocalyptic auguries appear
As frenzied *Snow* whips up the blizzard wild,
And midst it all in innocence and fear
Forgotten and forsaken, sleeps the *Child*.

Flora Electora

I know a place where dialectic flows
Where windswept *Clarke* and steel-eyed *Lilley* grows,
As, with the low *Lamont* they both entwine
The common *Hurd*, the heady *Heseltine*
Each binded by the rampant *Kinnock* root
And rosy *Prescott's* gaudy overshoot;
There, balmy *Ashdown* spreads its pollen round
And tiny media messengers abound
As, cautiously, the pale electors tread
Twixt tapestries of yellow, blue and red
For, lulled beneath this panoply of schemes
The serpent of ambition softly dreams.

Sic Sic

By these presents be it known
To all who bend before our throne,
Students, teachers, left wing heads,
Trendy academic reds,
That We, Ken Harry Clarke The Grand,
The Emperor of Cuckoo Land,
King of Moonshine, Prince of Schemes,
Lord of Mammon's wildest dreams
Will set in motion, heretofore,
The biggest shake up since the war:
A plethora of classroom skills
Devoid of philanthropic frills,
An end to airy fairy thoughts
Conceived in ancient college courts,
The death of careless negligence
And fickle philosophic sense.
Thus to you all We now impart
The secret of The Mentor's Art!
So be it written in this place
Our Sanctuary of doubtful grace,
Where, shivering from electoral frost,
We sit, enthroned, with fingers crossed.

The Ballad of Cool Hand Smith

The sun set on the old saloon
As nightly it was wont,
When Cool Hand Smith walked in the room
In search of Old Lamont.

He sneered around the smoky bar
And bared his shiny teeth
Then spat the butt of his cigar
At quivering Alan Beith.

'I've come to sing Lamont's lament!'
(A twinkle lit his eyes),
'I've come to claim a decade's rent
To pay for all those lies'.

Back of the bar in a solo game,
Old Norman studied hard
Then, careless of misdeed or shame,
Concealed a major card.

'The game is over!' Cool Hand cried
'Your time is nearly past.'
But swiftly Old Lamont replied
'It happened all too fast.'

Old Norman's fires were swiftly fanned,
He danced in wildest rage,
Then played his fatal final hand,
The ace of *minimum wage.*

Cool John stood still, as paralysed,
And leashed a fearful shout,
Then from his shadow sheath he prised
His manifesto out.

Poor Old Lamont fell to his chair,
He'd played his only trump,
With cold recession's wintry air
His body lay in slump.

Remember this and nothing more:
The coolest will survive —
This is the small screen's certain law
When the programme goes out live.

My Vote

If I wath very very old
And clever ath my daddy
I think I would be very bold
And vote for Mr Paddy;
That Mr Major'th far too nithe
And alwayth thayth ha! ha!
And daddy thayth that Mithter Thmith
Will thell uth to the thar.
No, Mr Paddy ith the one,
(The retht are far too shady)
And Mr Paddy'th penny tax
Will pay the dinner lady!

18

The Raving Loony's Charter

Well here it is, I promise you,
A bill to beat them all,
Total devolution
To town and county hall.
A thousand pounds per teacher
And cutbacks on the bumf,
Negotiated salaries
(At least three times a month).
Classes will be limited
To twelve point five per room,
With bold and biased graffiti
To beat the Tory gloom.
INSET will be twice a week
And guaranteed for fun,
At local leisure centres
(Or in the Dog and Gun).
There'll be no bloody Baker days
With rapid salary snacks,
No so-called twilight sessions
With inspectors on your backs.
Directed time will be no more,
We'll end each day at two —
Just like my new curriculum,
Entirely up to you!
Oh, it's a cracking charter,
Designed to make you glad,
But then I'm just a loony,
Starkers, raving mad.

What the Thunder Said

(The Survivors)

After the floodlight on powdered faces,
Tortured bravura in hot public places,
After the lies and the accusations,
Vanity, chimera, worthless quotations,
Promises surging from effluent fountains,
Perjury preached upon slag heaps and mountains,
After the slander and foul indictment,
Unctuous flattery, hollow excitement,
After the dinner, the wine and the dance,
The faithless seduction of artful romance,
Still, in the lurch of unfinished debate,
The orphans of rhetoric patiently wait.

Sirens and oracles, eerily white,
Solemnly slumber with dissolute eyes,
Each bearing scars of the long battle night,
(These are the nooses that once were their ties).
Dead to the world and their part in its pain,
Dead to the terrible cry of the watch,
Dreaming of chills and the showers of rain,
(Here is no water, only the scotch).

After the babble of eloquent fools,
Each with a specialised knowledge of schools,
After the underhand false exposure,
Who will now listen to warnings of closure?
And what is the message I hear on the air
Behind the new discourse of promise and care?
And why do they stand all so distant, aloof
At the mention of holes in a nursery roof?
After the final distasteful procession,
The cuts and the wounds blamed upon the recession,
Who plays for whom, and at what, on which side?
And who is the third party there at the side?
Our children will shore up the fragments again,
From dry sterile thunder, political rain.
Cracks and reforms may have driven them wild,
But a child, thank the Lord, is a child, is a child.

Begone dull care

From November 1990 to April 1992 — just eighteen short months — Kenneth Clarke succeeded in alienating the vast majority of teachers, trainers and officers in the Education service. Perhaps his greatest achievement was the removal of all liberal thinking from CATE, the Council for Accreditation of Training in Education. The effect was to remove power and influence from colleges and universities, and to throw yet another sector of the service into turmoil.
This, then, is his tribute.

C.

A Valediction

He arrived in the night with a pallor of white
Though his eyes were a sinister red,
And an odour arose from his ill-fitting clothes
Like a newly stripped hospital bed.

By the first light of day he had shuffled his way
To a narrow and poorly-lit street,
Where the neon-lit green of a seedy shebeen
Flashed in time to a decadent beat.

In its basement of booze he consulted his muse
With a Bavarian beer in his hand,
Then he swiftly began his dispassionate plan
To the tune of a dixieland band.

In his marketing brain it became very plain
That the school held the enemy's heart!
Though his maniac cry and delirious eye
Made the dissolute company start.

Then he thrust out his chin with a satisfied grin
And withdrew a small portable phone,
And he called every spy from Newcastle to Wye
(To the backing of bass and trombone).

Camouflaged by the band he gave out his command
To destroy all the reds in the state,
But the greatest of these to be brought to her knees
Was a redhearted redhead called Kate

Evil Kate possessed powers in the ivory towers
To influence social direction,
But the stranger well knew that a promise or two
Could infiltrate any affection.

In a very short spell he had set up a cell
In the temple of poor Katy's heart;
Very soon she lost sight of her left and her right,
And her principles drifted apart.

In his Tartuffian cape he completed the rape
With a tool of the coldest polemic —
Not content with his fill, he moved in for the kill
And her protests became academic.

With a smile on his face he deserted the place
And returned to his underground dive
Where, despite his acclaim, not a soul knew his name..
Just the stranger from M.I.5.

From the hospital ward to the polytech board
Every tale tells the terrible text:
That idealist thought can be easily bought—
And they say that the judges are next.

So he left in the dawn with a satisfied yawn
And none knew the size of his fee,
And while some called him stranger,
a lover of danger,
The rest of us just called him c . . .

The Peste

Aprille is the tyme for fooles
Sacken the techers, close the scoles,
Move the goles and change the rules,
Heigh ho for LMS!

Now it is biginnen Spring
Loude heer the Clerick singe
Privetisynge everything,
Nevere mynde the mess.

The Clerick gives us guarantee,
Grant maintayned and CTC
(These are not for you and mee)
Only for the beste.

In the village and the toun
Litel children wear a froun
Wryten al the answeres doun
In yet another teste.

Another yere of werk biginnes
Pestilence for al our sinnes
Surfeet paper filles our bynnes
Lorde wee are depressed.

See the scole inspectre there,
Worried eyen, greyen hair
The Clerick does nat seem to care
Tis just another jeste.

See the bynders on the floor
Key Stage One to Key Stage Four
Do notte sende us any more
Give us all a reste.

Aprille shoures starte to fall
Reyndroppes trickle doun the wall
The Clerick does not mynde at all
He's pleynly unimpressed.

The Cuckoo song is loud and rude
The litel children have nat foode
Lordes by the Holy Rood
He's fillynge up the neste.

See him Clarking al about
There is no shadowe of a doute
We have to throwe the cuckoo out
He trewely is a peste!

Pass the Cocoa Ken

We are the Oval Genie's
Happy girls and boys,
Through night and day
We work away
And never make much noise.

We spend our days in darkness
Just like busy bees,
We pull our forelocks
To His Clarkeness
Though we're on our knees.

Some teachers call him meanie,
Like the ones in Brent,
Others call him Mussolini
Call for ten per cent —
But we don't think the rise is teeny
Because we love you

OVAL GENIE!

We are happy girls and boys.

Nuts in April

A Seaside Medley

Here they are again
Happy as can be.
All the *delegatesof* the NUT.

See them stroll along
Every shape and sex
Even *Macavoyswearing*
Dayglo specs.

O we do like to be beside the seaside,
O we do like to be beside the sea,
O we do like to romp with our Reeboks on,
Far from the maelstrom of Key Stage One!
O we do like to be beside the seaside
Ruled by the moods of the tide,
Where we take our bat and ball
Into the conference hall
Beside the seaside, beside the sea.

Chorus: *(with feeling)*

Ooold Michael Fallon to the waall is gone!
In the lowest raanks you will find him;
He's put his ashes and his sackcloth on
But never moore will we miiind him:
He waaas the curse of ev'ry maid and maaan
But never mooore shall he grieeeve us;
For frankly nooobody gives a daaamn
Just so looong as he leeeaves us!

To conference they go,
To conference they go,
With every motion a virgin ocean,
To conference they gooooo!

The Winter Gardens Tale

(I come to bury teachers not appraise them... K. Clarke — attrib.)

In strange defiance of the natural laws
A smoother pattern calms the battered shores,
An easter peace is summoned by the bell
Of simple truths like Heaven versus Hell.
But who are these cavorting in the sand,
This miserable and battle weary band —
Their leader in his formal battle dress
Exhorts them ever onward in their stress.
'A little further' comes his fighting cheer,
'Nirvana lies beyond the Central Pier!'
At last the warriors sight their sacred home.
The haven of the Winter Gardens' dome.
With grateful thanks they throng into the hall
As for some ragged philantropic ball.
Through rank and file's mysterious warp and weft
Some weave to right but many more to left.
Thus settled in its delegated seat,
The Military heart begins to beat.
Small caucuses appear in tight knit bands,
Belligerent with radical demands.
Then all at once a scarlet Trojan Horse
Rides through the rhetoric with caustic force,
And Kenneth Clarke's ideal appraisal schemes
Explode in Blackpool's wildest fairground dreams.
The caterpillar cries from sleeping forms
Are barely heard within the violent storms,
And midst the fume of celebratory beer
Foul tempers drift up to the chandelier.
Executives cajole, refute, forewarn
With voices drowned by seas of popping corn,
And while the left flank, smiling, starts to mock
The facile grows into the rich baroque.
Some ride their hobby horses round and round
While others helter skelter to the ground.
The big wheel of opinion turns and turns
While other bums show old big dipper burns.
Old seaside donkeys bray their salty plans,

Ideas as old as rusty seaside trams,
Appraisal's progress takes a bitter blow—
(Described as kiss me quick and squeeze me slow).
The candy floss of proud appraisal quakes
Beneath the roar of rudely sucked milk shakes.
But then, at last, the bitter truth hits hard:
A boycott is no longer on the cards.
Within the old arcades behind the hall
Young militants express their bitter gall,
Curse quietly, bemoan the victory gone
'We've lost the battle.. still the war goes on'

Blackpool, Easter 1992.

30

... lastly through a hogshead
of real fire

God's Messenger

I am the Major's drummer boy,
I follow him to war,
I'll beat my drum till kingdom come
And evil is no more.

I am the Major's trumpeter,
I trumpet day and night,
I'll blow His name through wind and rain
To fight the moral fight.

Old Major called me to his side
And marched me up the hill;
He bade me cry with fervent eye
The glories of The Bill.

'Good fellow, John,' he beckoned me,
'Become my faithful Knight,
And you shall be, in Sanctuary,
Protector of the Light.'

And so I pledged my sabre's edge
To cut the Heathen lie,
And who disdains the grant maintained
Shall shrivel up and die.

Now I command a merchant band
Who march with heads erect;
And they shall ride at Major's side :
Their duty — to inspect.

O, we will ride the countryside
To give the peasants Choice.
(Damnation to democracy)
Rejoice, my friends, rejoice!

I am the Major's minstrel boy,
A master of romance;
Will you, won't you, will you, won't you
Join me in the dance?

Nunc Dimittis

Lo, in the barren seventh month
When many were abroad,
John Patten called His messengers
And raised a fiery sword.

Alone, aloof, on Sanctuary's roof,
Within a mystic cloud,
He spake with cold authority
A message clear and loud:

My people hear this covenant
And never bear a doubt,
Nor moan and cry like HMI,
For I shall cast ye out.

With well versed style and stealthy smile
He stole a modest bow
(A curl fell down his gentle crown
Upon his left hand brow).

This is My charter held for you,
Hear now the heavenly voice,
And kneel ye down at the trumpet sound
For I shall give thee Choice.

Then Patten's eye rose to the sky,
(Which all perceived as odd)
Come forth, he cried, *be sanctified,*
For I am next to God.

Henceforth I shall be known as Lord,
Let all pretence desist,
My deity is reassured
In next year's birthday list.

Thou shalt not cower to local power
Nor falsely overspend
But I shall lock thee in the tower
For decades without end.

Remember thou the Baker Day,
Vouchsafe directed time —
And should a surfeit come thy way
Remember it is Mine!

Be sure to honour all My laws
And all who govern thee,
Keep children locked inside your doors,
At least till half past three.

Thou shall not kill the golden goose
Which Sanctuary doth provide
By boosting rolls with idle souls
Attending for the ride.

Thou shalt not harbour lowly thoughts
Nor philanthropic lust,
Nor linger in the council courts,
For they are far from trust.

Thou shalt not choose thy multitude
Nor steal thy neighbour's prize —
Save for the shrewd with rectitude
Who wish to specialise.

Thou shalt not bear false evidence
About thy neighbour's tests
Except to My inspectorate
Whose judgement is the best.

And all the sinners saw his face,
Observed His shining blade,
Then left the presence of His grace
And trembled, sore afraid.

Apocalyptic samurai
Beset their journey home
As stormy blasts whipped up the sky
Like grey, prophetic, foam.

Lo, as they trudged along the track,
Demystified, alone,
They bore His gift upon their back,
A tablet made of stone.

Death by Soft Soap

In a small infant school, just outside Hartlepool,
There's a carnival beat in the air,
Where the staff, young and old, wear a countenance bold
And a brazen red rose in the hair;
While cupolas appear with designs cavalier
In such quaint little boroughs as Truro,
And the old rounders pitch has been callously switched
For a new game called Plaza del Toro.

In a nursery class on the dry autumn grass
Little children are chanting a stanza,
As the caretaker feeds the unnatural needs
Of a guinea pig named Sancho Panza.
There's a school in Devizes which now specialises
In risotto and red hot tortilla,
Where the pastoral schemes are designed around teams
Called Picasso and Santa Maria.

Yet another in Ryde has just recently tried
A peculiar opting out bid:
There's a bold matador on the headteacher's door
And a plaque which reads, simply, El Cid.
Every child in the land can now dance to the band
In abandoned flamenco and samba,
While the governors squeal on the financial wheel
With bloodcurdling cries of caramba!

Come now, let us all go where the hot pulses flow
In search of the new *libro blanco**,
Where Juan Patten leads us in radical deeds. . .
The kindliest general since Franco.
Let us sing *por favor*, there's pesetas galore
Stir our souls with an amontillado
We will march on and on with our leader Don Juan
Till we all reach the true El Dorado.

* white paper

35

The White Paper — a Demystification

I fear thee new millenium,
I fear thy aweful bell,
Thy specialised diversity,
Thy own selective hell.

I fear the market mockery,
The patronising voice;
Thy ill constructed rockery
Of non-existent choice.

I fear thy shameless metaphor,
Thy cold strategic soul,
The academic mystery
And *well defined goal.*

I fear thy ambiguity,
Thy emphasis on skills
Which augurs perpetuity
Of nameless social ills:

Autonomy, economy,
The secret victim's list,
Defined by Deuteronomy,
Administered in mist.

I fear the tremor through the land,
I fear the avalanche
When certain persons understand
The meaning of *carte blanche.*

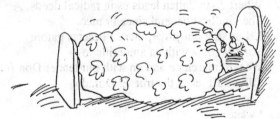

Why *not* shoot the messenger?

The Last Flight of the Shire Fighter

Flying through the fiscal flak,
Nervous in the semi dark,
Cost accountants at the back,
Radar jammed by Kenneth Clarke.

Infrastructure stretched to crack,
Skyline flecked with tracer mark,
Weaving in a fearful track
Atmospheric fireworks bark.

Turmoil! Turmoil! Swing to left!
Tremors shake the tragic flight;
Pyrotechnic warp and weft,
Pull the fortress to the right!

Turbulence till morning light
Rocks the fabled phoenix round,
Rising to horizon's height
Hurtling, screaming, to the ground.

Budget down at four o'clock!
Swing the mammoth crate around!
Screaming engines strain and knock,
Pilot's pulse begins to pound.

Climbing now in manic fear,
Warning lights begin to glow;
Silence from the bombadier,
Crackling on the radio.

Navigation hopeless now,
System locked in overdrive.
Time to take a final bow
Mayday.Mayday.
                    Dive!
                    Dive!
                    Dive!

Who's Who?

Leaving her paintings of azure and blue,
Dropping creations of delicate stitch,
Tightclad in tracksuit of tinselly hue,
Pretty Miss Porter appears on the pitch.

Nervously clutching a clipboard and pen
Passing a glance at a male colleague's shorts,
Jotting a note here and there, now and then,
Slowly she starts her appraisal reports.

Down in the hall with a desolate sigh,
Students perform in a science exam,
Dai Rugger Evans in blazer and tie,
Rubs down the cramp of an old injured ham.

Under the stairs in a cupboard-like room,
Appraisers and victims indulge in a joke;
Levity raises the aura of gloom
(For this is the haven of teachers who smoke).

Eons away in the conference suite
Far from the fierce educational fray,
Neighbourly headteachers cosily meet,
Mutual appraisal the plan for the day.

Stella the art student gives out a scream,
Quelling the quarrelsome year seven cry,
Struggling to stick to her aim and her theme,
Under the gaze of a cold mentor's eye.

Out through the window a governors' committee
Furtively measures the old mentor's skill,
Marking him down without favour or pity:
Performance inadequate —over the hill.

Local inspectors appear at the gate,
A building site clerk and a butcher's trainee,
Cautiously each asks the other his rate,
Carefully lowers the size of his fee.

Out of zone parents appear without warning,
Led by a deputy trained in intrigue,
Quoting a text that he learned in the morning:
'Swimming pool, science lab, top of the league!'

Others arrive claiming access to plans,
Details of funding and truancy rates;
Each with a charter clutched tight in the hand,
Feebly informed of the latest debates.

Back in the office the registrar trembles,
Borough accountants examine the books;
Nervously finance committee assembles
Hiding its horror with scholarly looks.

Faster and higher the fantasy flies,
Testing, appraisal, assesssment and pay,
Rhetoric, politics, eloquent lies,
Effluent gibberish, posturing play.

Who knows the purpose, the end of the plot,
Who planned this structure of imminent doom,
Who dares unravel the Gordian knot:
Who's testing who and for what and for whom?

Jazz

Well I woke up this morning
Didn't know where to start,
Somebody sent me
The targets for music and art
Sure looks to me
Like the horse is ahead of the cart.

Percussions and shanties
Fugues and sarabands,
Keyboards and descants,
Syncopating bands
Seems my education
Is turning into one night stands.

All kinds of music
All kinds of blues and jazz
Ellington, Waller
All that razamatazz
Till you get something new
You don't realise what you has.

Roll over baby
In your nursery cot,
Nanny's gonna take you
Down to Ronnie Scott's,
Teach you the score babe
Read those little dots.

Gonna take a journey
Round the swinging clubs,
Study the cultures
In the West End pubs
Then we're gonna sketch it
Just like Donatello or Stubbs.
Gonna take a look
At Dali and Pissaro
Dig old daVinci
Rave over H. Rousseau
Then we're gonna groove it
Onto the video.

Well, I woke up this morning
Didn't know what to do,
Woke up this morning
Feeling mighty blue
Just took the goddam paper
Flushed it down the loo....
                    yeah!

Shakespeare in Schools

But, soft! what voice through yon partition breaks?
It is the sound of Tina Turnbull's mum,
Whose horrifying bold iambic shakes
The structure of the frail curriculum.

A PE teacher wisely disappears
And swiftly climbs the highest wallbar rung,
As others tremble, breaking down in tears
For they have suffered Mrs Turnbull's tongue.

'Make haste!' the head implores her wretched team,
'Come quickly, follow me into the yard.
Do you not hear that dreadful Learlike scream?
The woman is demented with the bard!'

And, thereupon, an apparition rose,
A sight to turn the boldest critic grey,
Apparelled in Elizabethan clothes
Stood Mrs Turnbull ready for the fray.

'Behold, ye feeble, pedagogic pests!
I come to order what is rightly mine,
For all the latest evidence suggests
My Tina cannot scan a nursery rhyme!

What wasted hours has my poor childling spent
In mindless mathematical pursuit?
When she has never essayed to invent
A sonnet fit for medieval lute?'

The gentle head at last could stand no more
Her patience most unseemly pressed with strain
She strode across the hard gymnasium floor
And ordered Mrs Turnbull to refrain.

'Is this a parent here in such a state ,
An insubstantial charter in her hand?
Protect us from such ill informed debate,
Such propaganda rife throughout the land.

43

Confusion now hath made his masterpiece
This is the foullest folly of mankind:
If thou hast tears then give them sweet release
This charter's but a charter of the mind!'

'Then I am done' poor Mrs Turnbull cried
'I cannot jest at scars that cause me pain.
What, has the noble Mr Patten lied?
I'll never trust his silvered tongue again.'

At this the head grew pleasantly assuaged
And cast a sympathetic poet's eye,
For though at heart her righteous anger raged,
She could not bear to see a parent cry.

'Be easy now, your painful guilt is wrong,
To call you Mistress Cuckold would be cruel.
Come join with us in loud triumphant song:
For Shakespeare *lives* in Tina Turnbull's school!'

School is for Kids too

Syllabus A

Safely numbered in our seats,
Persecution starts;
Set square, compass and protractor,
Sadly sinking hearts.

Cold instructions, regulations,
Questions clear as mud,
Last year's fifth year's old graffiti
Carved in this year's wood.

Compound interest, weird equations,
Strange, perplexing sums,
Agonised and unrevised,
Tortured, deadened bums.

Ticking clocks and talking teachers
Punctuate the hell;
Pity us pathetic creatures:
Ring the bloody bell!

Another of Life's Sweet Mysteries

There comes a time in every life
When all the power of the Gods
Descends imposing cruel strife
Upon us petty mortal sods;
When carrot peelings block the sink
And curry sauce bedecks the wall
When politicians make you think
There is no point to life at all.
But nothing beats the pure distress,
The fearful pagan cabaret,
The unexplained psychotic mess
Of infants on a windy day.

Performance Art

Wayne you have to be a fairy
Come on Julie take it off
I can't do it Mrs Cleary
My mum says I've got a cough
Move about now Rachel Hewson
Wave your hands now don't just stand
Mind that dustbin
Put your shoes on
I'm not holding Bernard's hand
Please miss I've got pollen fever
David do not kiss the wall
No you're not an Easter leaver
Robin give me back that ball
There's the bell
Come back this minute
God it's hot
This floor is hard
I wish the school exams were finished
I hate drama in the yard!

Now we are theven (muthic)

I really love my muthic clath
We have it in the hall,
The nithetht thing about it ith
There are no boyth at all.
I don't like drumth or bagpipthe,
I think they're far too loud —
I'm really betht at thinging
Ethpethially in a crowd.

My teacher likthe my thinging voithe,
She thayth I'm trying hard,
Exthept thomethimthe she makthe me go
And practithe in the yard.
I find thome wordth quite difficult,
Like largo and vibrato —
And I don't know why she'th chrithtened me
A little othtinato.

PSE Poem

Pre-menstrual tension can get you detention
Especially in Science and Maths,
Feeble excuses have very few uses
And protests provoke only laughs.

Abuse and perversion create a diversion
And words from the pastoral head,
But mostly they moan and we're left on our own,
So we're sniffing the Tippex instead.

Summer Relief

The unofficial opening of the football season

Once more it is the violet hour
When harrowed heads lock up their files,
And abdicate the key of power
To registrars with weary smiles.

Relieved at last of termly tasks
The final tour of duty starts.
Discarding managerial masks,
With lightened step and lighter hearts.

Adjacent in the network room
A deputy, with anxious frown
Makes final changes in the gloom
Before he shuts the system down.

With thoughts of next years option list
He leaves the keyboard and the screen,
His soul obsessed, a floppy disk
Worn out by endless plans and schemes.

The head of art in sweet decay
Surveys the scene of wear and waste
Regards the tattered old display
The pencil shavings, paint and paste,
The dried up cacti, faded flowers,
Abandoned in improper haste.
The evidence of fruitless hours,
A tapestry of childish taste...

Music teachers without choirs
Sing of solace and release
Cataloguing lutes and lyres
Stunned by unaccustomed peace.

In the staffroom (hardly swinging)
Party jokes become more rude
Loud debate gives way to singing
Lyrics loud and slightly lewd.

Mugs with slogans raised up high
Replace the elegance of glass
Old teachers, one reads, *never die:*
They only lose their class.

Quite distant now, the eager campers
Career along in motorcades,
Packed with maps and Tesco hampers,
Heading for the healthy glades.

Down in the town they drown their sorrows,
Wringing out the strain and stress,
Drinking thoughtless of tomorrow:
Coldly cursing LMS.

Evening falls and tempers tire;
Termtime tension soon abates,
Fury loses all its fire,
Hell is locked within its gates;

Now returns Midsummer's Rule
Careless cleaners stand aloof;
As truant boys return to school
To claim their footballs from the roof.

Overheard on the Beach

When I go back to thchool next week
I'm in Mith Taylorth clath,
We're taking our eleven pluth
I hope that I don't path,
Coth my betht friendth are bottom thet
And *alwayth* make me laugh
(And Thaint Therethath uniform ith really rather naff).

A Postcard from Devon

Here at last a kind of safety
Saves us from the darts of school,
Feet in sandals, sand in coffee,
Children, friendly, in the pool.

All are measured by the T shirt,
Surfing skills and paddling style;
Weird culottes and off-the-knee skirts
Raise an eyebrow and a smile.

Fearless of the cold Atlantic,
Careless of September's chill,
English poets grow pedantic,
Scanning coastlines with a thrill.

Gingerly, the awkward caper
Down the shingled, rocky reach;
Kleenex is the whitest paper
On this distant Devon beach.

Overheard on the Beach (2)

O God is there just one more week of this!
Reclining in forgetful summer bliss,
Just one more week before the steady climb
Up next year's academic one in nine,
Before the fall from energetic heights
Into the trough of late November nights,
The twilight in the departmental room
Beset by innovation's dismal gloom.

So far away from all this hazy glee,
The sun, the sand, the sky, the sighing sea.
So far the sacred, calm, untroubled peace,
So brief this mindless, paperless release.
Just one more honest, self-indulgent week
Before the slick return to doublespeak.
Then pour me out one more quadruple gin . . .
Come, blow ye winds, let Autumn term begin!

September is the saddest month

Thermal Verse

Piping down the valleys wild,
Pumping plunder from the sea
Piping prices to the sky
Singing songs of thermal glee.

Piping profits through the air,
Paying for my style and class,
Pocketing the lion's share,
Don't you think it's just a gas?

Withdrawal Method

Under the swirling of Autumnal wrist
Bearing the memory of alien skies
Teachers return to tutorial lists
Gingerly wince at the bloodcurling cries.
Clearing their desktops of last year's intentions:
Overbold schemes that have long ago died,
Lesson notes shaped with outrageous pretensions —
All washed away by reality's tide.
Memories of sunlight in Torremolinos,
Fruitful Sangria by sparkling pools.
Love affairs played in the Spirit of Calvados —
All fade away in the cold light of school.
Fists filled with biros, hearts full of heaviness,
Each leads the way in a pastoral dance
Hiding the guilt of their blatant unreadiness
Chained once again to curricular chance.

Back to Maastricht

Now September's dull sensation
Draws a veil on summer fun,
Governmental exhortation
Clouds all memories of the sun;
Thoughts of sacred summer mornings
Fade like friendly forest mists,
Dulled by bureacratic warnings,
Convoluted schemes and lists.
Gone the easy conversation
Round the sizzling barbecue,
Clichés coined by every nation:
Ravioli? Fleur de chou?
Gone the cheery morning meeting
Mid the tents of red and green,
Euroteachers Eurogreeting,
Happy in their Euroscene.
Guten Tag. Bonjour. Good Morning.
Ich bin lehrer. Je suis prof.
Grüssgott. Hi there! *Buena sera.*
For six weeks you have it off?

Now the mistral drives its forces
Hard across the Côte Sauvage;
Wild apocalyptic horses
Beat upon the soaking plage.
Lightning from the Callac mountains
Lays the battered coastline bare.
Motorways like streams and fountains
Flood from Brest to St Nazaire.
Sarajevo thunder crashes,
Shadows cast a sombre hue;
Boreas bestirs the ashes
Floating in the barbecue.
Clearings fill with oily vapours
Damp cicadas sing in vain,
Sly mosquitos cease their capers,
Downward falls the heartless rain.

In the schoolyard, tyres deflated,
Mudsplashed Ford and Peugeot,
Sadly roofracked, GB plated,
Park with nowhere else to go.

Möchten Sie a chocolate biscuit?
Moi, je préfère Brooke Bond Tea.
Danish Pastry? **Liebe Maastricht!**
Roll on 1993!

September Assignment

Write about 500 words on one of the following:
  i)   My summer holiday
  ii)   Adolescent relationships
  iii)   Pop Music

Deep in the heat of a camp site rave,
Little Tina Turnbull dances the night,
Filled with the thrill of a chemical wave,
Flying in the flash of fluorescent light.
Driven by the rhythm of a high speed laser,
Pulse pumped hard with a pocket full of pills,
High as a kite, sharp as a razor,
Stuttering steps in the strobe light stills.
Boogying close as the beat drives harder,
Hippity together to the disco door,
Sinking in the seat of a clapped out Lada,
Scrabbling for the condoms on the cold car floor.
Back to the caravan at half past three
(Parents paralytic on the double divan)
Worried over syphilis and HIV,
Pimples that appeared instead of a tan.
Packed next morning sitting in the car,
Eyes shut tight with her walkman on,
Dreams of a foetus in a marmalade jar,
Childhood, babies, holidays gone.
Rainclouds form on the fading hill,
Wipers start to squeak on the fly-stained screen,
Eyes turned cold in the wintry chill
As the radio plays sweet little sixteen.

Theven and a bit

My thithter'th in the thecond year,
She that her that latht week,
It wathn't very difficult
I think they've got a cheek.
When me and Thuthan did *our* that
The teacher went quite thpare
(She'th got thuch nithe bifocalth now,
And lovely thilver hair).
If every tetht getth leth and leth
I'll be in theventh heaven —
There won't be any tethting left
When I become eleven.

Lingua Peripatetica

Two cold days after bonfire night
Depression falls again,
Another year of hopeful light
Extinguished by the rain,
Another year of sacrifice
To academic dreams
Discarded by the careless dice
Of local council schemes.

Two days again from bonfire night
It's time to take a jog,
To struggle in the endless fight
With the mongrelspaniel dog.
Look Andrew there's a vowel blend!
Perhaps again it's not.
I think I'm going round the bend,
Or maybe it's a plot.

Well it's off to Holy Trinity
And back to old St Bridget's
Where Doreen has Divinity
And Tracy has the fidgets.
Poot Jasmine Iqbal once again
Has lost her reading book,
My words of comfort pour in vain,
She spurns my caring look.

And nobody knows its my birthday again
Two days from the gunpowder plot,
I'm part time and peripatetic:
Thanks a lot Kenneth Clarke,
Thanks a lot.

Via Triviale

'. . . building bridges between contemporary experience and the classics. . .'

O magic Street! O comfortable chair,
Where tales unfold like aimless mountain sheep.
O Weatherfield, devoid of ravelled care
That couches us in easy dreamless sleep;
Where greasy Betty fills the empty plot
With petulance and flighty twists and turns,
While jolly Jacko raises up his pot
And downs the Rover's dwindling returns.
Consider how our painful life is spent,
The icy wind of truth upon the cheek,
Then ask how any critic could resent
This uncouth pleasure just three times a week?
The maudlin Mavis, Derek's dear delight,
Young Curly Watts and witless, boring Ken
Fill up each Monday, Wednesday, Friday night
While Rita groans beneath the ghost of Len.
What Shakespeare, Dickens, Wordsworth or Marvell
Could match this most pedestrian conceit?
Let Milton sing of Sampson in his Hell:
True agony is Coronation Street!

a right royal poem

It's awfully bad luck on Diana
She's having a rough ride with Prince
He does nothing but falter
When she pulls on his halter
And just starts to whinny and wince.

It's awfully bad luck on Diana
Her stable's a terrible mess
And her terrible fall
At the Royal Windsor Ball
Has appeared in the worst of the press.

It's so soon after Andrew's disaster
And mama's in a terrible spin
It's a bit like the porkie
They told about Yorkie
Oh, how can a poor royal win?

Even Edward looks set for some slander
Fancy taking a job on the stage!
Such an aesthetic pose
Really gets up one's nose
(And his father is quite in a rage) .

O it's awfully bad luck on Diana
Perhaps she should contact Nick Ross?
There's a man, without doubt,
Who can sort it all out ...
Frankly, darling, I don't give a toss.

True stories

Response
(to Adrian Henri's inclusion on the 1994 English Literature Syllabus)

Do you remember, Adrian,
The Merseyside savannahs,
The afternoon I spoke to you
In drunken Peter Kavannagh's?
I asked where you where going,
You told me 'to the match'
Then swiftly threw a bitter
Down your wide and fulsome hatch.
'I do not understand 'I said
'Why your poems never rhyme.'
You laughed: 'I write them in my head,
In the toilets at half time!'

Reathonth for Reading

I read a thtory in the hall
And everybody thmiled,
They even heard it at the back
Where all the chairth are piled.
That wath tho nithely read Janine!
The chair of governorth thaid.
But how I wish, I do tho wish
I knew jutht what I'd read.

Teachers I have Known

I'll always remember Alister Beatty
Expert in classical felt pen graffiti,
A practised exponent of urinal rhyme
Until he ran dry for a noticeable time.
'I'm slipping,' he said 'all the muses are gone',
As he slid from his stool with Byronic aplomb.

The Baker's Tale

I used to be a miller man,
A master of the seed,
I ground my corn from night till morn
To meet the Thatcher's need.

The Thatcher was a comely lass
With powerful allure,
She forced me speak two times a week
The science of manure.

I was the Thatcher's miller man,
I ground her dirty grain,
And with a laugh I kept the chaff
To feed my Gerbil's brain.

My Gerbil gained enormous size
And ate the holy grail,
So I was sent to implement
My policies in jail.

And now I'm painting tulips
To sanctify my soul,
And hold my piece in sweet release
In the Valley of the Mole.

Footy Poem for the Fourth Term

At the end of the day it's a nightmare scenario,
Moveable goalposts and uneven fields,
Strategies planned by a slick impressario,
Careless of tackles and steel studded heels.
Boardroom behests in a daily epistle,
Avarice stirred from the shareholders' box;
Quick fire commands from the very first whistle,
Heartless instructors in tight gartered socks.
Push up attendances (whip, stick or carrot)
The bigger the turn out, the better the pay:
Politics, rhetoric, sick as a parrot ...
Sisyphus rules at the end of the day.

'God bless, us one and all'

Santa Clarke's Last Visit

It was late in the night
When I heard on the roof
The uncertain step
Of a suede leather hoof,
As I turned round my head
I perceived in the gloom
A strange looking character
There in the room.
He was dressed all in fur
From his head to his tail
And his breath held the flavour
Of seasonal ale.

A gigantic bundle
He held in his fist —
Its weight made him stagger
And walk with a list.
His eyes all atwinkle
His cheeks like a cherry,
His laugh was infectious
And festively merry;
He held a cheroot
In his wide grinning teeth
And its smoke filled the room
Like a funeral wreath.

With a wink of his eye
And a studious frown
He twisted his cumbersome
Sack upside down;
Then he danced a quick step
With a skip and a caper
As he filled up the nursery
With pencil and paper!
He smiled to himself
With benign satisfaction,
And clumsily sprang
Into furious action.

As he shot up the chimney
And vanished from sight
I heard his small voice
From the snow covered night:
They may not be much folks,
But be of good cheer,
For you'll need all that stuff
For the testing next year!

(And they did).

Advent

The bells of waiting Audit ring,
Accountant's candles burn again,
And Cooper Lybrand's angels sing
A cold monastic Christmas strain;
While clerks sit warm by Whitehall's glow,
Impervious to the coming snow.

Christmas at Sea
or
The Wreck of The Gerbil

'Twas on a frosty Christmas night
When cold electoral winds did blow,
And seagulls made erratic flight
To flee the salty hail and snow.

Down through the craggy cliffs of Cowes
The wicked winter whipped the waves,
Chastised the Jolly Gerbil's bows
With threats of cold and watery graves.

No hopeful morning star appeared
To light the loathsome stormy skies,
And every sailor bowed with fear
Beneath the surly captain's eyes.

Upon the bridge old Captain Clarke
Urged ever greater rates of knots,
While pressed recruits down in the dark
Lay shivering in their nauseous cots.

These were the teachers, sixties trained,
Who failed to make appraisal's grade,
Opponents of the grant maintained,
Political, and overpaid.

These were the knaves who fought the Act,
The weak who could not do the job,
The long-haired and the anoraked,
The liberal left and loony mob.

Their fitful dreams were troubled sore
By words like freedom, market, choice.
Their souls were sickened to the core
By echoes of the Master's voice.

From many a school this motley crew
Had joined the sad and tragic cast,
Hard pressed in redeployment's queue,
They fell before the Gerbil's mast.

The Gerbil crashed and changed her course,
One teacher gave a startled cry,
Woke from a dream of dread remorse
Repeating 'No more TVEI . . .'

In swinging hammock, Evan Jones
Lay crying from his lyric soul,
Lamenting in his Celtic bones
A silence mute as mountain coal.

'No more tuition!' Evan groans.
'No songs to still the stormy sea!
Bring me your harps and brass trombones,
I'll give you lessons all for free!'

Once more the Gerbil changed its course
And every hand fell out of bed,
A thunderous crash of cosmic force
Filled all their minds with morbid dread.

This horror raised their fearful eyes
Up to the creaking salty beams
Where stretching timber's eerie sighs
Competed with the blizzard's screams.

A tiny teacher, Joyce by name,
Walked slowly to the only light
Where 'neath its ghostly yellow flame
She whispered softly, 'We must fight.

For years we've suffered Clarke's abuse
His rhetoric and coarse asides,
He says our teaching is no use...
I'll bear no more his roughshod rides!'

At this the gentle militant
Grew glorious in the feeble light,
And like a seasoned adjutant
Displayed her English teacher's might.

All hands stood still with anxious stare
The Gerbil lurched another time,
Then Joyce's passion filled the air
In most appropriate classic rhyme:

'It's time to lose our fear of Clarke,
To disenchant his petty rage,
Like mushrooms we are in the dark,
With verbal sewage as our wage.

It's time to disregard that frown
Deformed by Panatella smoke,
To tell him that we will not drown,
And show The Gerbil as a joke.

We must not fear his lightning wit,
His slanders heavy as a stone —
Declare him as a hypocrite,
Whose empty praises make us groan!

Let us return to common land
Where love is long and nonsense short.
Come, shipmates let us make our stand,
And take this vessel back to port!'

Three rousing cheers rang through the room,
Old Evan sang a canzonet,
But Joyce's voice possessed the room,
It seemed she had not finished yet...

'Who stands this cold auspicious night
In revolution's noble war
To put the tyrant Clarke to flight,
Will be remembered evermore.

When parents, children, every one
Will freely join their hands and say
Rejoice the market force is gone
Defeated on this Christmas Day.

Full fathom five the Gerbil lies,
Its Captain's bones deep in its bows,
This the noblest glittering prize,
Upon the sea bed just off Cowes!

Wait, something strange is in the air,
I sense a salty pungent smell!
The muses warn us to beware,
Hear now, there is the middle bell!'

Each eye then turned away from Joyce,
A shiver ran down every spine,
For they had heared another voice...
Midshipman Fallon, soaked in brine!

'What words are these?' he wryly smiled,
'Do I hear loony lefties call?'
His lips were thin, his pupils wide:
'Be glad you've got a job at all!

You'll never make much headway here,
You teachers don't know how to fight.
The Captain says you're just small beer...
A union that cannot unite!!'

He laughed and turned his evil back,
But ere he reached the starboard stair
His head received an awful crack
From Evan with a wooden chair.

'Avast ye bureaucratic fool!'
Bold Evan sang with lyric glee.
'Begone you governmental tool,
Before I throw you out to sea!'

Old Fallon slithered up the stairs,
Pursued by Eggar (Gerbil's mate)
While Captain Clarke showed little care,
Quite heedless of his colleague's fate.

'Come now' he smiled, 'I've done no wrong.
I've given you parental choice,
I've made your governing bodies strong,
I've given you . . . O hello Joyce.'

His adam's apple rose and fell,
His eyebrows arched in sudden fear.
'Twas then he heard the Lutine Bell,
The warning that his end was near.

'This Christmas time your turn has come,'
Said Joyce, 'Ken Clarke, you're fortune's fool.
Just think on all that you have done
In college, nursery and school.'

The slender soul then grabbed his arm
And turned him quickly on his heel;
Disdaining all his sickening charm
She lashed him to the spinning wheel.

'Now master of this fated ship,
Change course again, but just once more,
And let us make a final trip
Directly back to Reason's shore.'

Just then a faint familiar cry
Came downward from the mizzenmast,
The naked eye could just descry
A creature from the distant past.

'A sail! A sail!' came down the yell,
'Twas young MacGregor, cabin boy.
The captain's face grew grim as hell:
'Then let's go to it. Ship ahoy!'

With fearsome strength he spun the wheel
And caused the bows to sharply turn,
While all the teachers danced a reel
And stumbled to the open stern.

The Gerbil rose, then shuddered down
As timbers fell upon the deck.
And like a sad symbolic gown
The ensign draped the captain's neck.

Now, hopelessly, the Gerbil span
Like some impotent, dying whale
And round the bridge the captain ran,
Declaiming loud 'A sale! A sale!

I can't resist a market chance,'
He spake with fearful quivering lip,
Then gave the skies a manic glance:
'I mean to privatise this ship!'

Back in the stern the rebel band
Pushed out the boats with anxious hearts,
Then carefully (and hand in hand)
They pulled away to safer parts.

By dawn a calmer Christmas breeze
Conjoined a strange unseasonal sun,
And all who scanned the level seas
Perceived the Jolly Gerbil gone.

The first daze of Christmas

The lights in District Office dim
And lone advisers walk the street,
Their faces in expressions grim,
Their pallor white as winding sheets;
While lights bedecking County Hall
Say Merry Christmas to us all!

Old Major's Christmas Message

It was Christmas Eve in Downing Street
And the hour was growing late
As old Lamont with frozen face
Glared glumly at the grate.

'Stoke up the fire 'ere we retire,'
The mighty Major cried
'I feel a bitter North East wind
Around my nether side.'

'The coalman has not called this week,'
Lamont lamented long,
'I fear there will be little cheer
To light our festive song.'

It was a tiny troupe indeed
To greet the joyful morn,
With business suits all baggy kneed
And shiny elbows worn.

The common Hurd without a word
Had long since gone to bed,
A chilly shroud of Maastricht cloud
Still hanging round his head.

Wild Heseltine had long resigned
With melancholy eyes,
The fault lines of a nation's mines
Writ large upon his eyes.

Ken Clarke stood up and raised his cup,
A sparkle in his eyes,
'I know a party game,' he said
'It's called I *privatise*.'

'Stud poker is a pleasant game,'
The Chancellor replied.
'My John prefers Monopoly,'
(Came Norma's soft aside.)

From deep within the ingle nook
There came an eerie voice:
'Come take a lesson from my book
To help you to rejoice.

I have the very recipe
To charm away the chill.
Sit back, relax, I'll read to you
A chapter of my Bill.'

As bold John Patten took his feet,
A mystery occurred,
The company fell fast asleep
Before he spake a word.

The languid torpor of the don
Had every soul beguiled,
And as John Major slumbered on
He dreamt he was a child.

Within this warm and wishful world
The minor Major smiled
As old familiar tales unfurled
In adolescent styles.

The memories flowed fast and deep —
The Christmas pantomime —
Where myriad minor characters
Sang songs in Santa's mine.

The lady from the LEA —
A Mrs Appleseed,
Who made the costumes for the play
And taught him how to read.

The little chap was bathed in bliss
And stared with wondrous awe
Until he heared a solemn voice
Behind a study door:

'Young Major is a minor brain,
I'm sure you will agree
That he will find it quite a strain
To take the GCE?'

Another said 'His mock exams
Are really quite unstable,
I'd rather not have *his* results
Upon the school league table!'

The slumbering Major starts in fear,
A stately timepiece chimes
And over and again we hear
John Patten's turgid rhymes.

'Diversity, Capacity,
Ability to Choose,
Inspection with Rapacity — '
'Have we run out of booze?'

The rhythmic spell is cast to Hell
By Kenneth Clarke's dismay,
Then Major towers to fullest power
And rips the Bill away.

Page after seeming endless page
He tears with manic craze,
Then casting them upon the coals
He blows a mighty blaze.

A Phoenix from the festive flame
Flies far across the snow
And every school hears Major's Rule:
John Patten's Bill must go!

Christmas 1992